# ISRAEL

## Susie Hodge

W

FRANKLIN WATTS
LONDON • SYDNEY

First published in 2008 by Franklin Watts

© 2008 Arcturus Publishing Limited

Franklin Watts
338 Euston Road
London NW1 3BH

Franklin Watts Australia
Level 17/207 Kent Street, Sydney, NSW 2000

Produced by Arcturus Publishing Limited,
26/27 Bickels Yard, 151–153 Bermondsey Street, London SE1 3HA

Series concept: Alex Woolf
Editor: Alex Woolf
Designer: Ian Winton

Picture credits:
Corbis: cover *left* (Jon Jones/Sygma), cover *right* (Jerome Sessini), 10 (Bettmann), 12 (David Rubinger), 13 (Reuters), 14 (Yonathan Weitzman/Reuters), 15 (Annie Griffiths Belt), 16 (Ricki Rosen), 18 (Ted Spiegel), 19 (Reuters), 20 (Wolfgang Kumm/dpa), 21 (Jim Hollander/epa), 22 (Ricki Rosen/Corbis Saba), 23 (Peter Turnley), 24 (Reuters), 25 (Reuters), 26 (Ed Kashi), 27 (Alex Rozkovsky), 29 (Jim Hollander/epa), 31 (Richard T Nowitz), 32 (Kerim Okten/epa), 34 (Justin Lane/epa), 36 (Jim Hollander/epa), 37 (Reuters), 38 (Richard T Nowitz), 40 (Jim Hollander/epa), 42 (Ronen Zvulun/Reuters), 43 (Reuters).
Rex: 30 (Israel Sun).
Shutterstock: 6 (Kavram), 7 (Mary Lane), 11 (Joshua Haviv).

The illustrations on pages 8, 9, 15, 27, 28 and 39 are by Stefan Chabluk.

Cover captions:
Left: An Orthodox Jew prays at the 'wailing wall' in Jerusalem.
Right: Children play on the beach of Ashdod on Israel's Meditarranean coast.

A CIP catalogue record for this book is available from the British Library.

Dewey Decimal Classification Number: 915.694

ISBN 978 0 7496 8210 1

Printed in Malaysia

Franklin Watts is a division of Hachette Children's Books, an Hachette Livre UK company.
www.hachettelivre.co.uk

# Contents

# CHAPTER 1

# ✡ Introduction

Israel is a small country in the Middle East that occupies a narrow strip of territory at the eastern end of the Mediterranean Sea. Known to many as the Holy Land, Israel is located in a land of central importance to three of the world's major religions – Judaism, Christianity and Islam – and in 1948 it was established as the world's only Jewish state. Since then, from being a sparsely occupied country, its population has increased over eight times to nearly seven million. The sheer number of new inhabitants have generated many changes in the country – social, economic and cultural.

## PHYSICAL GEOGRAPHY

Area:
  *total:* 20,770 sq km
  *land:* 20,330 sq km
  *water:* 440 sq km
Highest point: Har Meron – 1208 m
Lowest point: Dead Sea – 408 m
Land boundaries:
  *total:* 1,017 km
  *border countries:* Egypt 266 km, Gaza Strip 51 km, Jordan 238 km, Lebanon 79 km, Syria 76 km, West Bank 307 km
Coastline: 273 km

Source: CIA World Factbook

The Negev Desert takes up most of the southern half of Israel. It is a rocky desert full of mountains, sandy plains, wadis (dry riverbeds that flow briefly after rain) and deep craters.

This is a hillside in northern Galilee. Some parts of this mountainous region reach heights of over 1,200 metres. In between the highlands lie small, fertile valleys, dotted with orchards and vineyards.

## Three continents

Israel is situated at the meeting place of three continents – Africa, Asia and Europe. It is part of Asia, while neighbouring Egypt belongs to Africa. The long, narrow country contains fertile valleys, barren deserts, large lakes, rocky mountains and scenic coasts. It measures some 450 kilometres north to south, from the northern village of Metulla on the Lebanese border to the southern city of Elat on the Red Sea. At its widest, near the desert city of Beersheba, Israel is only 180 kilometres from east to west.

A sandy Mediterranean coastline forms the entire western side and its land borders meet the four Arab countries of Lebanon, Syria, Jordan and Egypt. In the south, a huge triangle of land known as the Negev Desert narrows at the port of Elat on the Gulf of Aqaba. It also contains two lakes that are so enormous they are called seas: the Dead Sea and the Sea of Galilee. Both are fed by the River Jordan. The Sea of Galilee is a freshwater lake and the Dead Sea is the world's saltiest lake.

## Valley beneath the Sea

At the bottom of the Dead Sea is the Great Rift Valley, a massive crack in the Earth's crust that runs from Syria to southern Africa. It runs almost in a straight line from north to south, along the entire eastern edge of the country. Israel's major rivers are the Jordan, Qishon, Yarqon and Yarmuk. The River Jordan forms part of the country's eastern border, dividing Israel from the country of Jordan. Most of the other waterways are seasonal streams called wadis, which flow for part of the year and dry up for the rest. Since 1967, Israel has also governed some other areas of land, known as the occupied territories. These comprise the Golan Heights in the north-east, the West Bank in the east and (until 2005) the Gaza Strip in the south-west. Jerusalem, the capital city, is 800 metres high in the Judean Mountain Range.

**This chart shows the climate of Jerusalem. Located in Israel's central upland area, temperatures here are marginally cooler than on the Coastal Plain.**

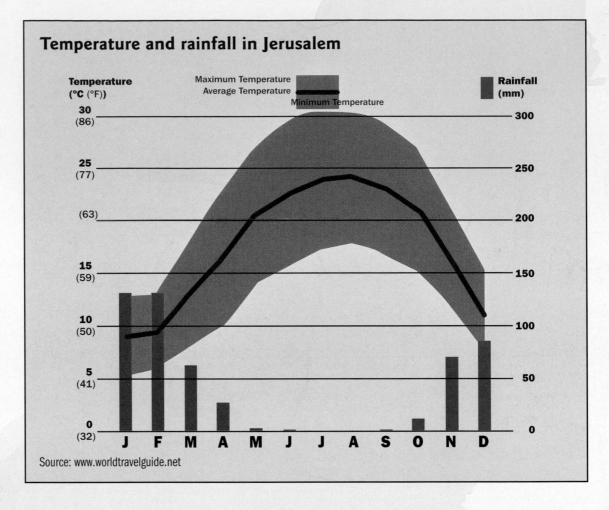

Temperature and rainfall in Jerusalem

Source: www.worldtravelguide.net

## Climate

Israel has a Mediterranean climate, with long, hot, dry summers and mild, wet winters. Between May and September there is hardly any rain at all, and about 70 per cent of the year's rain falls between November and February, mainly in the north and west. In high mountain areas, such as Jerusalem, some light snow occasionally falls in winter. Summers are hot and fairly dry in the mountainous regions, but are more humid on the Coastal Plain. Sometimes, in late spring and autumn, hot, dry, dusty air moves in from the east and sends temperatures soaring. This wind is known as the *sharay* in Hebrew and the *hamsin* in Arabic.

## Culture

Israel is a unique blend of ancient and modern – the old lands that are described in the Bible and the new, vibrant, developing nation. Its culture reflects the diversity of its immigrant population, who have brought their customs and traditions from many different places, including Eastern Europe, Russia, the Middle East and North Africa. Although Israel is officially a Jewish state, people of other faiths also live there. Around 76 per cent of the population is Jewish (comprising around a third of the world's Jews), 16 per cent is Muslim, and the rest is made up of Christians, Druze and Bedouin. Each community preserves its own culture, including religious worship, food, art, literature and social contact. Because the two main groups of people are Jews and Arabs, the official languages of the country are Hebrew and Arabic. Many Israelis speak both languages, as well as English. Many others still speak the languages of the countries they came from.

# Conflict

The conflict between Arabs and Jews in the land now known as Israel occurred long before the country's establishment in 1948. In the 1890s, European and Russian Jews, known as Zionists, started to settle in Palestine, and clashes soon began with the Palestinian Arab inhabitants. Since Israel was founded in 1948, the disagreements have continued. The Palestinians, having lived on the land for many centuries before the Zionists arrived, believe that the land is theirs. The Jewish claim is based on the fact that, in 1947, the United Nations (UN) partitioned the land into two states, one Jewish, the other Arab. Many Jews also believe that Israel was promised to them by God, as stated in the Bible. Although the conflict is essentially an argument about who owns the land, it is also a religious conflict between Jews and Muslims. Violence and wars have erupted frequently since 1948 and a peace settlement has proved difficult to find.

**Israel is bordered by Egypt to the south-west, Syria and Jordan to the east and Lebanon to the north. Its most important river, the Jordan, flows from the north through Lake Hule and Lake Kinneret (also known as the Sea of Galilee or Sea of Tiberias), and empties into the Dead Sea 411 metres below sea level – the world's lowest land elevation.**

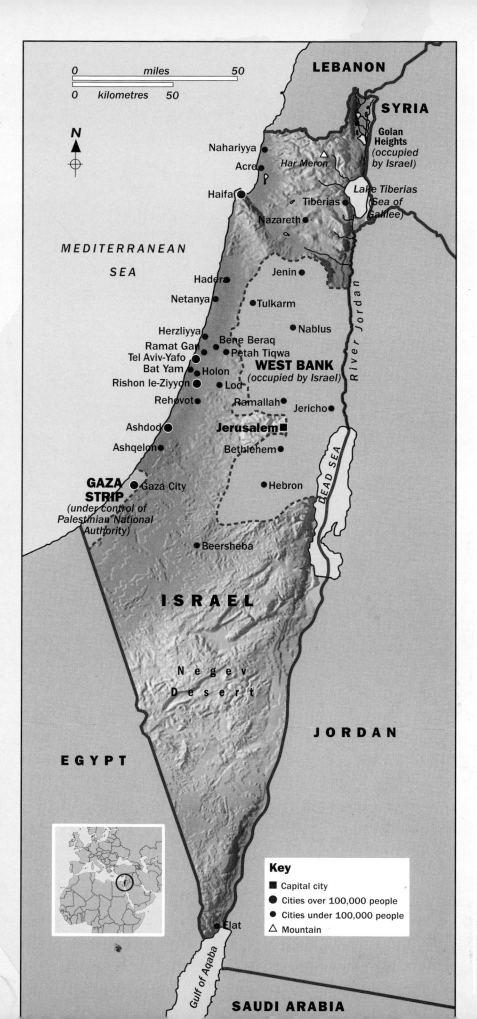

# CHAPTER 2

# ✡ History

In about 1500 BCE, several early Hebrew tribes settled on the land now known as Israel. Some 500 years later, a king called David united the tribes and formed the kingdom of Israel. David's son Solomon helped to make Israel rich and powerful by setting up trade links with other lands. He used some of the wealth to build a great limestone temple in Jerusalem. When he died in 928 BCE, quarrels broke out between the north and south of the country and it split into two kingdoms: Israel in the north and Judah in the south. In 722 BCE, Israel was destroyed by the Assyrians, who were one of the great empires of the Middle East at the time.

## Invaders

Later, Judah was conquered by a series of powerful invaders, including the Babylonians (586 BCE), the Persians (538 BCE), the Greeks (333 BCE), the Romans (63 BCE) and the Byzantines (330 CE). The Babylonians exiled the Judeans (known as Jews), but in 538 BCE the Persians allowed them to return home. The Jews rebuilt Jerusalem, including the great temple. In 70 CE, after the Jews rebelled against Roman rule, the Romans burned the

**Jews frequently faced persecution in the places where they settled. This engraving shows the expulsion of Jews from Spain in 1492. Only those Jews who were willing to convert to Christianity could remain.**

temple to the ground. After this the Jews began to leave Judea (as the Romans called their land) and move elsewhere. This was the start of a mass scattering of Jews around the world known as the Diaspora. By the eighth century CE Jewish communities had been established as far east as China and as far west as Spain.

## CASE STUDY: JERUSALEM

Jerusalem is holy to three religions. To Jews, it was the site of Solomon's Temple, but all that remains of the Second Temple, destroyed by the Romans, is its Western Wall. It is holy to Christians because many events in Jesus's life occurred there. Jerusalem is also the third holiest city of Islam after Mecca and Medina in Saudi Arabia. Muslims believe that the Prophet Muhammad rose to heaven from Jerusalem to receive God's word. Jerusalem's walled 'Old City' is divided into quarters – Muslim, Jewish, Christian and Armenian – demonstrating its importance to different cultures and religions.

## Sacred place

Under the Byzantines, Judea was renamed Palestine and it became an important centre of Christianity, being the place where Jesus of Nazareth, the founder of Christianity, lived and died. In 638, Palestine was conquered by Muslim Arabs. Muhammad, the founder of Islam, was said to have ascended to heaven from the Dome of the Rock in Jerusalem, and so Palestine also became a sacred centre of Islam. The land remained almost continuously under Muslim control until the fall of the Ottoman Empire (a Turkish Muslim empire) in 1918.

Throughout their history, the Jews had suffered persecution in the lands they settled. During the 1890s, there was a rise in anti-Semitism (hatred of Jews) in parts of Eastern Europe and Russia. Many Jews believed the only way to protect themselves was to create a separate Jewish state. The Zionist movement was established with the aim of founding a Jewish state in Palestine.

In the Six-Day War, Israeli forces captured East Jerusalem from Jordan. The Paratrooper Brigade captured Temple Mount – a particularly sacred place for Jewish people, which includes the Western Wall. Here, Israeli paratroopers stand at the Western Wall shortly after its capture.

In 1920, two years after capturing Palestine from the collapsing Ottoman Empire, Britain established a mandate (rule) over the country. The British government had promised the Palestinians independence and had also vowed to create a Jewish national home in Palestine. Neither Arabs nor Jews wished to be ruled by Britain – both desired an independent homeland. Discord between the two peoples became intense.

## The state of Israel

The movement to create a Jewish state attracted worldwide sympathy following the Holocaust, when over six million Jews were slaughtered by the Nazis during World War II. In 1947, Britain wished to end its mandate, and the United Nations (UN) planned to split Palestine into two states, one for Jews and one for Arabs. In May 1948, the British departed from Palestine and Jewish leaders declared the founding of the state of Israel. War broke out as six Arab states invaded, determined to destroy Israel at birth. But after 15 months, the Jews had won control of 75 per cent of Palestine. Transjordan (modern Jordan) took over the West Bank, and Egypt took the Gaza Strip. Around 726,000 Palestinians fled Israel and settled in the West Bank, Gaza and neighbouring Arab states. Just 150,000 remained in Israel.

## Continuing conflict

In 1964, the Palestine Liberation Organization (PLO) was founded with the aim of replacing Israel with a Palestinian Arab state. In June 1967, fearing imminent invasion, Israel launched attacks on Egypt, Syria and Jordan. In just six days, Israel

## CASE STUDY: THE SIX-DAY WAR

In 1967, Egypt, Jordan and Syria gathered troops close to the Israeli borders, sent UN peacekeepers away and blocked Israel's access to the Red Sea. Israel retaliated with strikes that lasted for six days. Over that time, Israeli troops captured Gaza and the Sinai Peninsula from the Egyptians, the Golan Heights from Syria and the West Bank from Jordan. This more than trebled the territory under its control. Following the Six-Day War, many Palestinians began to focus their support on the PLO.

organized by Hamas, an Islamist terrorist group calling for the destruction of Israel. Then, in 1993, Israel and the PLO signed a peace deal. The Israelis agreed a staged withdrawal from the occupied territories, and a Palestinian Authority (PA) was set up to take civil control there. But the peace process stalled in the late 1990s and in 2000 a second intifada began. In 2005, Israel withdrew its settlers and troops from Gaza, and the territory subsequently fell under the control of Hamas.

captured substantial territories from all three countries, including Gaza and the West Bank. Over 750,000 Palestinian Arabs living in these two territories now found themselves under Israeli authority. In 1973, Egypt and Syria struck Israel again during the Jewish holiday of Yom Kippur. Israel drove them back but was shaken by the surprise attack.

In 1987 the first intifada broke out. This was a Palestinian rebellion against Israeli military occupation in Gaza and the West Bank. It was

**A masked Palestinian in Jerusalem's Old City prepares to hurl a rock from a sling in December 2000 during the second, or al-Aqsa, intifada. The uprising was sparked by a controversial visit by Israeli politician Ariel Sharon to the al-Aqsa Mosque compound of the Temple Mount in September 2000. One of the mosque minarets can be seen in the background of this photo.**

13

# CHAPTER 3

# ✡ Social Changes

When it was founded in 1948, Israel's population was 806,000. Today, it is nearly seven million. Much of this rapid growth has come from immigration. The government has actively encouraged Jews to settle in Israel, and most of its population are Jewish. Before 1948, Jews were a minority in the land.

## Traditional inhabitants

Apart from Jews, there are also long-established communities of Muslims, Christians and Druze living in Israel. There are around a million Muslim Arabs, most of them Sunni. This includes around 170,000 Bedouins – wandering Arab tribes who move around the south of the country in search

### POPULATION

Population in Israel today: approx 7 million
Ages:
    *0-14 years:* 26% (male: 858,246; female: 818,690)
    *15-64 years:* 64% (male: 2,076,649; female: 2,046,343)
    *65 years+:* 10% (male: 269,483; female: 357,268)
Life expectancy:
    *total population:* 80 years
    *male:* 77 years
    *female:* 82 years
Ethnic groups:
    *Jewish:* 76% (of which Israel-born: 67%; Europe/America-born: 23%; Africa-born: 6%; Asia-born: 4%)
    *non-Jewish:* 24% (mostly Arab)
Source: Israel Ministry of Foreign Affairs

of grazing land for their herds of sheep, goats and camels. The Christian Arabs number around 113,000. Most belong to the Greek Catholic, Greek Orthodox and Roman Catholic Churches. The Druze, who number around 106,000, follow a religion similar to Islam, although they broke away from mainstream Islam some 800 years ago. This provoked persecution from other Muslims, so they moved to hidden places in the mountains where they still live today.

**A young Bedouin boy in the northern Negev. Some 70,000 Bedouins live in about 36 villages in this region. Most of these villages do not receive basic facilities such as water, electricity or health care.**

A Sephardic family picnics in a West Jerusalem park, celebrating the holiday of Maimuna. This is the day following the end of Passover and is in honour of Moses Ben Maimon (Maimonides) a distinguished medieval Sephardic scholar.

# New arrivals

Although most people in Israel are Jewish, not all have the same outlook. Because they have come from very different parts of the world, many of their customs and traditions vary. These differences have sometimes caused tensions within the Jewish population. The two main Jewish communities are the Ashkenazim and the Sephardim. Ashkenazi Jews originated in Central and Eastern Europe and were the first settlers. Sephardic Jews arrived later, from the Middle East, North Africa and around the Mediterranean. The Ashkenazim began moving to Palestine during the late 19th and early 20th century, escaping Russian persecution.

The Nazi threat caused more to flee to Palestine in the 1930s and 1940s. Ashkenazi traditions, including music, art and political ideas, became integral to Israeli culture.

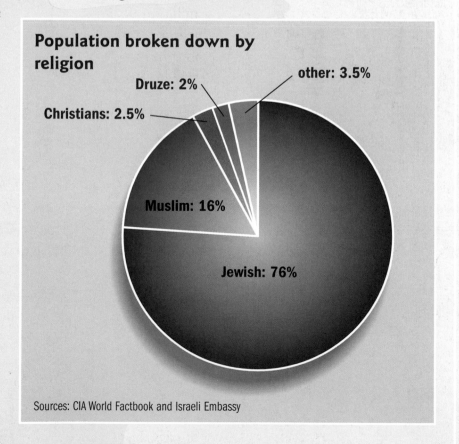

Population broken down by religion

Druze: 2%
other: 3.5%
Christians: 2.5%
Muslim: 16%
Jewish: 76%

Sources: CIA World Factbook and Israeli Embassy

This chart shows the religious make-up of Israel's population. Some 2.75 million Jews have emigrated to Israel since 1948, greatly expanding the Jewish community.

After 1948, over 700,000 Sephardic Jews were expelled from Arab lands. Most went to Israel. They had darker skin, wore different clothes, sang different songs, ate different foods and had a different outlook on life than the Ashkenazi. Most Sephardic women stayed at home and raised large families, while Ashkenazi women often worked in jobs outside the home. The differences caused tension between the two communities, but recently they have become much closer. Ways of life that older generations did not understand are accepted by younger Israelis as simply aspects of their country's rich, diverse traditions.

Today, a million Israeli citizens – one in five Jews in the country – are immigrants from the former Soviet Union, following its collapse in 1991. They include many accomplished musicians, scientists and professors, who have enriched Israeli cultural and intellectual life.

**Ethiopian Jews arrive in Israel in March 1990. New arrivals were sent first to an 'Absorption Centre' where they were provided with clothing, assigned housing and given training to help them fit into Israeli society, including lessons in Hebrew. The centres also organized group visits to important religious sites, such as the Western Wall.**

## COMPARING COUNTRIES: POPULATION DENSITY

Israel is a crowded country, with a population density twice as high as France and nearly as high as the UK:

Australia: 2 per sq km

France: 100 per sq km

Israel: 200 per sq km

Japan: 320 per sq km

United Kingdom: 231 per sq km

United States: 25 per sq km

## Operation airlift

To escape persecution, entire communities of Jews have been taken to Israel in numerous dramatic airlift operations. In 1949, Operation Magic Carpet flew the 49,000 Jews of Yemen to Israel. Between 1950 and 1952, Operations Ali Baba, Ezra and Nehemiah transported some 243,000 Iraqi Jews to Israel. And in 1991, 19,000 Jews from Ethiopia were flown to Israel in Operation Solomon.

The Ethiopian Jews could not communicate with the people of their new host country, they had little education and were used to life in a far less developed land. The Israeli authorities took steps to help them find homes and jobs. A television station broadcasts the news in their home tongue of Amharic, and social workers have introduced special programmes to help them to integrate. However, there remains no Amharic-Hebrew dictionary and, while many younger Ethiopians are doing well, older immigrants often feel isolated.

## Arab communities

The Arabs who live in Israel usually consider themselves to be Palestinian by nationality and Israeli by citizenship. Most are descendants of those who remained in the country after 1948. Nearly half the 1.3 million Israeli Arabs live in the northern Galilee region. They have the right to vote and to receive social services, and they attend government-funded schools where they are taught in Arabic about their history, religion and culture. However, this has served to reinforce divisions between themselves and the Jewish majority, and tensions remain between the two communities.

## Urban centres

The first Jewish immigrants, arriving in the 1890s, settled mainly along the lush Mediterranean coast. Today, this coastal strip is the most densely populated part of Israel. Some Jews and many Arabs live in farming communities, but most Israelis live in cities. Over half reside in the three biggest cities of Jerusalem, Tel Aviv and Haifa. Some 92 per cent of Israelis live in settlements of 2,000 people or more.

Jerusalem, in the Judean hills, covers 126 square kilometres and has a population of about 690,000. For the first 19 years of Israel's existence, Jerusalem was a divided city. Then, in 1967, Israel captured East Jerusalem from Jordan, uniting the city under Israeli rule.

Tel Aviv, on the Mediterranean coast, was originally two cities – Tel Aviv and Jaffa – that have since joined up. Jaffa is an ancient port, while Tel Aviv was founded in 1909 by Jewish immigrants. Tel Aviv-Jaffa has developed into Israel's leading commercial, industrial and cultural centre. It comprises the country's largest urban region, covering 150 square kilometres and with a population of over 3 million.

Haifa, to the north of Tel Aviv, is Israel's main port and another important industrial centre. It has a population of around 948,000. Beersheba, the largest city in the Negev, has a population of 184,000.

## The kibbutz and moshav systems

Many of the first Jewish settlers from Eastern Europe were idealists who wished to create a fair and equal society in which people owned wealth and property collectively. In 1909 they founded the first kibbutz (plural: kibbutzim) near the Sea of Galilee, based on these principles. More followed and there are now over 250 kibbutzim. They are farming communities whose members work not for their own profit but for the community as a whole. Committees govern kibbutz life, taking care of everything, including finance, education and health. Members share all property and responsibilities equally. They do not earn money, but are given housing, meals, education, health care, holidays and a personal allowance. Many young people from other countries spend time on kibbutzim, joining in with the work and lifestyle.

Teenage volunteers from abroad help with the apple harvest on a kibbutz. They work hard in exchange for food, somewhere to sleep and the chance to forge new friendships.

### FOCUS: EDUCATION IN ISRAEL

Education in Israel is free for children up to 18 years old, and compulsory for five to 16-year-olds. About 80 per cent of schoolchildren speak and write in Hebrew and about 20 per cent study in Arabic. There are religious schools which offer a full curriculum but place a special emphasis on Jewish studies. Vocational schools teach skills such as electronics or cooking to older students, and agricultural schools provide training in farming. Israel has eight universities and numerous colleges of higher education.

The moshav (plural: moshavim) is similar, but inhabitants are more independent. Several villages are grouped around a central town in a moshav. Each family owns their own home and farmland. Unlike kibbutzim, moshav residents make their own decisions and cook and eat in their own homes, but the community shares the cost of equipment and supplies, as well as the profits from the sale of produce. The first moshav was established in the Jezreel Valley in 1921 and today there are about 450 moshavim. Today, both kibbutzim and moshavim participate in industry, services and tourism, as well as farming. About three per cent of Israel's inhabitants live on them, but together they produce about a third of the entire country's food requirements.

## Settlements

Since 1967, numerous Jewish settlements have been built in the occupied territories, often in areas where Jews lived in ancient times. The largest number of settlements have been built in the West Bank (known historically as Judea and Samaria). The Palestinian inhabitants are resentful of the Jewish settlers, and settlement building remains a major source of tension between the two communities.

In 2002, following a spate of suicide bombings by Palestinian extremists from the West Bank, the Israeli government began building an eight-metre-high concrete 'security fence' around the Palestinian-controlled parts of the territory. The barrier has attracted international condemnation. Most Israelis are in favour of it as suicide bombings have decreased since its construction. Palestinians see the fence as a way for Israel to sieze more Palestinian land and control the Palestinians who live there.

**A Palestinian boy rides his bicycle next to a temporary section of the security fence (soon to be replaced by a permanent concrete version) in July 2003. The Jewish West Bank settlement of Har Homa (near Bethlehem) can be seen in the background. The UN regards this as an illegal settlement.**

# CHAPTER 4

# ✡ Political Changes

The state of Israel is a democratic republic. The right to vote extends to every citizen over the age of 18. There are numerous political parties, representing a wide range of opinions. All the parties compete to be elected to the Israeli parliament, the Knesset. This is a single-chamber legislature of 120 members, each elected for a maximum term of four years. The Knesset debates and votes on legislation and approves budgets and taxes. The prime minister is the most powerful person in Israeli politics and is usually the leader of the majority party in the Knesset. Together with his or her cabinet, the prime minister decides policy and proposes legislation to be debated by the Knesset.

**The General Session Hall of the Knesset. The seats are arranged in the form of a menorah (Jewish candelabra). The Knesset meets for at least eight months a year. It enacts laws, elects the prime minister and oversees the work of government.**

Kadima party leader Ehud Olmert (left) embraces Shimon Peres, the Israeli president, following Kadima's victory in the March 2006 parliamentary elections. Olmert formed a government and became prime minister on 4 May, having been acting prime minister since January when his predecessor, Ariel Sharon, suffered a stroke.

## Political parties

For much of its recent history, Israeli politics has been dominated by two parties: Labour and Likud. Labour supports a welfare state, equal rights for minority groups and a negotiated agreement between Israel and the Palestinians. Likud believes in free enterprise, keeping the occupied territories and adopting a more forceful approach to foreign affairs and security. Neither party has ever achieved an absolute majority in the Knesset and have only ever ruled in coalition with smaller parties.

The Labour-Likud stranglehold on Israeli politics was broken in November 2005 when Prime Minister Ariel Sharon resigned from Likud and started a new party, Kadima, supporting peace with the Palestinians and strengthening Israeli security. In the March 2006 elections, Kadima (now led by Ehud Olmert after Sharon suffered a stroke) became the largest party in the Knesset, winning 29 of the 120 seats, which allowed them to form a government in coalition with some smaller parties.

## COMPARING COUNTRIES: POLITICAL SYSTEMS

### US Government

The USA is a federal republic with a written constitution. Certain powers are vested in the federal government and other powers are assigned to the individual states that make up the federation. Its legislative branch, known as Congress, consists of two separate assemblies: the House of Representatives and the Senate. The executive branch consists of the president and the cabinet. The president is both head of state and head of government.

### Israeli Government

Israel is a democratic republic. Unlike the USA it is run as a unitary state, with power concentrated in central government. Israel has no formal constitution, but a set of nine Basic Laws. Its legislative branch, known as the Knesset, has one house. The executive branch consists of the prime minister, the president and the cabinet. The prime minister is head of government. The president fulfils the ceremonial role of head of state and holds little political power.

Many of Israel's smaller parties are religious, with particular appeal to the Ashkenazim or Sephardim. Religious parties are too small to form a government (they generally occupy some 12-15 per cent of Knesset seats between them), but act as pressure groups promoting orthodox Jewish views and the Jewish settlement of the occupied territories.

An Arab Israeli woman places her vote in the ballot box at a polling station in Abu Ghosh, a town west of Jerusalem. Arab Israelis are granted the same political rights as all other Israeli citizens.

## Arab Israelis

Arab Israelis have always been classed as citizens of Israel with equal rights. They run the political affairs of their towns and villages and vote for their representatives in the Knesset. Arab Israelis have served in government positions and are increasingly involved in the political system.

Israel's 1948 Declaration of Independence promised that Israel would 'ensure complete equality of social and political rights to all its inhabitants irrespective of religion, race or sex. The only legal distinction between Arab and Jewish citizens is that Arab citizens do not have to serve in the army as other Israeli citizens do. This is because of the links between Arab Israelis and other Arabs involved in the Palestinian-Israeli conflict.

Despite government efforts, there remains a deep divide between Arab and Jewish communities, and many Arab Israelis feel discriminated against in terms of jobs and housing. Since 2000, the Israeli government has attempted to improve the lives of Arab Israelis by establishing job training courses and building more schools, sports halls, community centres and health clinics.

## The Armed Forces

Israeli Defence Force (IDF) comprises the country's army, navy and air force. Having had to defend the country in five major wars and many other clashes, the IDF is one of the most battle-trained armed forces in the world. Over the years, as well as defending Israel, the IDF has taken on other functions within Israeli society. It has provided services, including education, for new immigrants, assisted in disadvantaged areas and responded to emergency situations in the civilian sector.

### CASE STUDY: THE WEST BANK

In 1968, the first Jewish settlers began moving onto formerly Arab land in the West Bank. As more settlements were built, Palestinian resentment towards Israel grew. After talks between Israeli and Palestinian negotiators in Norway in 1993, it was agreed that the Palestinians should regain civilian control over the West Bank (military control remained with Israel). So Israel began returning control of parts of the territory to the newly formed Palestinian Authority (PA). By 1999, when the peace process ground to a halt, over 29 per cent of the West Bank was under PA control. People living in PA-controlled areas can no longer vote in Israeli elections.

**A Palestinian boy talks with Israeli soldiers in the West Bank city of Hebron on the day the agreement was signed to hand civilian control of the city to the Palestinian Authority.**

At 18, all eligible men and women are conscripted to the IDF. Men serve for three years, women for 21 months. New immigrants may serve for shorter periods. Arab citizens are not conscripted (see above), but may volunteer. After mandatory service, each soldier can be called up for up to 39 days a year until they are 51. In February 2006, the Israeli Defence Ministry announced plans to reduce compulsory service for male soldiers to 28 months, and ultimately to two years by 2010.

## The peace process

In 1978, Israel negotiated an historic peace deal with Egypt, the first between Israel and an Arab state. However, no progress was made on peace between Israel, its other Arab neighbours and the PLO until the early 1990s. Face-to-face negotiations between Israeli and Palestinian representatives began in 1991. One result of this was a peace treaty with Jordan in 1994, ending

46 years of war. Talks with the PLO led in 1993 to the Oslo Accords. Under the terms of this treaty, Israel began withdrawing from the occupied territories and civil authority passed to the newly formed PA. Many conservative and religious groups within Israel opposed the peace plan, claiming that Israel was giving up land without any guarantees of security. Militant Palestinian groups were hostile to any form of peace deal with Israel, as they believed Israel had no right to exist.

In the late 1990s, the peace process stalled as Islamic militant groups Hamas and Islamic Jihad began using suicide bombers against Israeli

**Israeli prime minister Yitzhak Rabin (left) shakes hands with PLO chairman Yasser Arafat as US president Bill Clinton looks on, following the signing of the historic Oslo Accords at the White House in September 1993.**

A bus burns following a suicide bombing near the Israeli city of Netanya in September 2001, injuring 17 people. Such bombings have hardened Israeli attitudes and set back the peace process.

civilians and Israel recommenced building Jewish settlements in contravention of the treaty. Renewed efforts to achieve peace in 1998 and 2000 were unsuccessful and in September 2000, Palestinians began the al-Aqsa intifada. Israeli security forces struck back, invading and reoccupying West Bank towns that had been handed over to the PA.

## International support

Israel has attracted both support and condemnation from other countries around the world. One of its strongest supporters has been the USA, which has supported Israel since 1949 with financial loans and charitable contributions. Around 33 per cent of the US foreign aid budget goes to Israel, even though Israel comprises just 0.001 per cent of the world's population. The extent of US aid to Israel has become increasingly controversial as some Americans believe it is harming US interests in the Middle East and adding to Arab resentment towards America. Israel also receives aid from Germany. The largest part of German aid has been in the form of compensation payments to victims of Nazi atrocities. Since 1948, German assistance has amounted to around US$31 billion.

### FOCUS: THE ROAD MAP

In 2002, an international group consisting of the UN, the USA, the European Union and Russia gathered to discuss how peace could be achieved. In April 2003, the plan for peace between the Palestinians and the Israelis was set out in a proposal known as the 'road map for peace'. The road map asked for the Israelis to stop building settlements and for the Palestinian Authority to adopt democratic reforms and abandon terrorism. Little progress has been made with the road map, and the Hamas takeover of Gaza in 2006-7 seemed to make peace appear even less likely. Nevertheless, many international observers continue to regard the road map as the most hopeful route to peace in the region.

# CHAPTER 5

# Economic and Environmental Changes

**B**ecause of the on-going conflict, a large proportion of Israeli government spending is devoted to defence and counter-terrorism. High levels of immigration have also necessitated substantial expenditure on housing and social welfare. Despite these pressures, Israel is considered one of the most advanced countries in the Middle East in terms of economic development, and most Israelis enjoy a high standard of living. Israel has few natural resources, and must import many of its raw materials, yet it has thriving industrial and agricultural sectors.

## Farming

Today, nearly 40 per cent of Israel's land is used for farming – over three times the cultivated area in 1948. Much of the increase in farmed land has been due to the draining of swamps and irrigation of desert land so that crops could be grown and animals reared on it. Israeli farms are highly mechanized and intensive. Consequently, they employ just 2.5 per cent of the workforce, yet provide around 75 per cent of Israel's domestic needs. Because of the country's shortage of fresh water, Israeli scientists have pioneered new methods of obtaining water for use in irrigation. Techniques include drip irrigation (which delivers water directly to crop roots), the purification of sewage water, cloud seeding (dispersing chemicals in clouds to induce rain) and desalination (removing salt from seawater).

Israel's warm climate and sophisticated agricultural techniques allow its farmers to produce a variety of crops all year round. During winter, while European farms lie dormant, Israel

**A farm worker buries an irrigation pipe in a field in the Negev. Since 1964, the Negev has been irrigated by water carried by pipeline from the Sea of Galilee and the River Jordan.**

Work on a new gun ship, for use at the forthcoming Olympic Games in Athens, nears completion at a shipyard in Haifa in 2003. The Israeli firm won the 100-million-dollar contract to build three ships in the face of competition from several leading shipyards around the world.

becomes one of Europe's primary sources of agricultural produce. Major crops include vegetables, cotton, beef, poultry, dairy products, citrus and other fruits. During the late 1980s, thousands of citrus trees were cut down because of water shortages, but today citrus fruits are once again the country's biggest agricultural export.

## Industry and services

Israel has undergone a rapid industrial expansion since 1948, thanks largely to the arrival of large numbers of skilled workers and professionals from Europe and North America, as well as overseas financial aid, and the government's policy of investing in research and development. Major industries include refining imported oil, manufacturing aircraft, chemicals, construction materials, electrical goods and machinery. Another important activity is diamond cutting. Before 1948, most diamond cutters were based in Amsterdam and Antwerp. Today, Israel is the world's top exporter of cut and polished diamonds.

**This chart shows the breakdown of Israel's gross domestic product by sector. The biggest contributor to GDP is the service sector, which includes public services, business and financial services, retail, transportation, communication services and tourism.**

The largest part of the Israeli economy is the service sector, which contributes around 67 per cent of the nation's GDP, or gross domestic product (the total value of all goods and services produced by a country in a year). Most people in this sector are employed by the government or by state-owned businesses. A major area of activity is the provision of housing, education and training for the immigrant population.

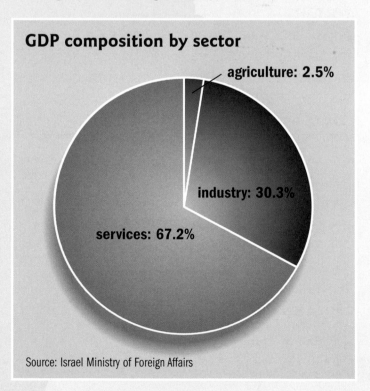

**GDP composition by sector**

agriculture: 2.5%
industry: 30.3%
services: 67.2%

Source: Israel Ministry of Foreign Affairs

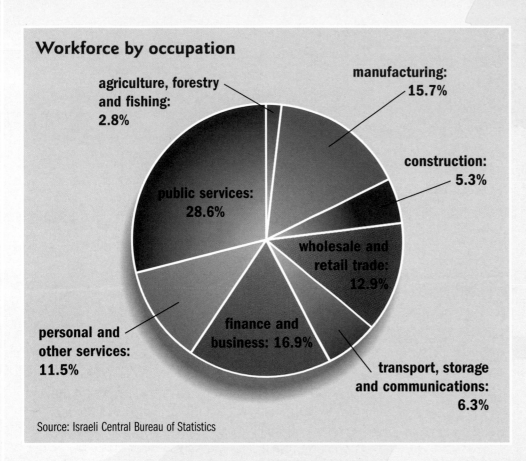

## Workforce by occupation

agriculture, forestry and fishing: 2.8%

manufacturing: 15.7%

construction: 5.3%

public services: 28.6%

wholesale and retail trade: 12.9%

personal and other services: 11.5%

finance and business: 16.9%

transport, storage and communications: 6.3%

Source: Israeli Central Bureau of Statistics

This chart shows the composition of the Israeli workforce. The largest proportion of employees work in the public sector or for government-owned businesses. This sector has shrunk since the 1980s when the government began privatizing many of its businesses.

°In the 1980s, to help stimulate economic growth and reduce spending, the Israeli government began selling many state-owned businesses to private investors. However, the government remains the country's largest employer, especially in the public services sector.

## Technology and trade

In 1973 the Israeli government set up the Office of the Chief Scientist (OCS) to help companies to pay for research and development into new products and industries. The investment has paid off, and since the 1980s Israel has enjoyed significant success as a manufacturer of high-technology products such as agricultural and electronic equipment, telecommunications and weapons systems. Israeli companies have also initiated major advances in electronics – particularly in the fields of medicine, nuclear power and computers. Israel also has a successful

chemical industry, producing fertilizers and drugs from its few natural mineral resources, including bromine, potash, phosphates, manganese and sulphur.

Due to its shortage of natural resources, Israel must import more than it exports. In 2004, it had a trade deficit of US$3 billion. Much of this annual shortfall is paid for by grants and loans from the USA and other governments, donations from Jewish organizations, bank loans and funds brought in by immigrants.

The nation's main trading partners are the European Union and the United States. Chief imports include chemicals, grain, iron and steel, petroleum products, rough diamonds and textiles. Israel's main exports are chemical products, citrus fruits, clothing, electronic equipment, fertilizers, polished diamonds and processed foods.

## COMPARING COUNTRIES: THE ECONOMY

### Germany

Germany's main imports include raw materials, metal, machinery and chemicals. Major exports include cars, machinery, metals and chemical goods. Farming provides 90 per cent of Germany's nutritional needs. Chief industries include aircraft, computers, electrical and electronic equipment, food processing, forestry and fishing, mining, cars, railway equipment and textiles. Germany is first in the world in generating wind power and is the main exporter of wind turbines.

### Israel

Israel's major imports include fossil fuels, raw materials and military equipment. Leading exports include fruits, vegetables, pharmaceuticals, software, chemicals, military technology and cut diamonds. Farming provides 75 per cent of Israel's nutritional needs. Chief industries include metal products, electronic and biomedical equipment, processed foods, chemicals, transport equipment and diamond cutting and it has developed advanced technologies in software and communications. Israel is a global leader in water conservation.

## Poverty

Israel's economic prosperity has enabled most of its citizens to enjoy a high standard of living. Yet some 1.5 million Israelis live in poverty. Many of the Sephardic Jews who arrived in large numbers during the 1950s found it hard to adapt to Israel's mainly Ashkenazi culture. With their North African or Middle Eastern origins, most Sephardic Jews lacked a European education and so found it hard to compete for the top jobs. The Arab Israeli community found themselves similarly disadvantaged. Consequently, the majority – though not all – of Israel's senior business and political leaders are from the Ashkenazi community.

**An elderly Palestinian woman begs outside the Lion's Gate by the walls of the Old City of Jerusalem, as Palestinian Muslims leave the al-Aqsa Mosque. According to a 2006 report by Israel's National Insurance Institute, 53 per cent of impoverished families in Israel are Arab Israelis.**

Between 1960 and 1990, Israel's population more than doubled and its built-up area quadrupled. It is estimated that the population will reach about eight million by 2020 and its urban area will more than double again. Nearly 20 per cent of the land is reserved for nature conservation, but construction and development have taken their toll on the environment and the Israeli government recognises the need for a more sustainable approach.

## Water shortage and pollution

Preservation of the country's scarce water sources is possibly the greatest challenge facing Israel. Many of its major rivers have been contaminated by agricultural or industrial waste, or sewage from local towns and cities. For example, the Kishon River, which flows through Haifa, has been severely polluted by raw industrial waste from nearby chemical factories. The Ministry of the Environment has set up several river restoration projects and improved sewage treatment plants, and polluters face strong penalties. By limiting the development of coastal industry and resorts, the government is also taking steps to protect the Mediterranean and Red Sea coastlines.

The combination of a limited fresh water supply, contamination of existing water sources, densely populated urban areas and highly intensive irrigated agriculture, has encouraged a policy of highly efficient and innovative water usage. All possible water resources are exploited, including springs, groundwater reservoirs and the River Jordan. The Israeli National Water Carrier project carries water from the Sea of Galilee in the north to areas where it is needed. When it was started in 1953, the project's main goal was to provide irrigation for the Negev region. Today, however, 80 per cent of the water drawn from the Sea of Galilee is used for drinking water.

These storks were part of a flock of over 150 that died from poisoning after landing in a pool contaminated by waste from an industrial plant near the town of Dimona in the Negev.

Heavy traffic clogs the streets next to the beach in Tel Aviv. The number of vehicles in Israel nearly doubled between 1995 and 2005, significantly increasing air pollution. The government has introduced measures to encourage people to switch to public transport.

needs. The government hopes to exploit one of its major natural resources, bright sunlight, and expand the use of solar power. Today, all new buildings are equipped with solar water heaters.

## Air pollution

Rapid technological developments, higher living standards, increased population density, new industrial plants and a dramatic increase in the number of cars have all intensified Israel's air pollution problems. So in 2005, the government passed the Clean Air Act, which set up an air-quality management programme to monitor air pollution levels throughout the country.

## Energy

Israel has few natural fuel sources, and depends on coal and oil imports to meet most of its energy

### FOCUS: WASTE AND RECYCLING

Because of Israel's increasing population, solid waste disposal is a problem. Until recently, hundreds of unregulated rubbish dumps were scattered throughout the country. In the early 2000s the government ordered the closure of all unlawful tips and the waste transferred to a few authorized landfills. Most of the country's waste is now concentrated in 15 sites and about 85 per cent of it is disposed of or treated in ways that minimize air pollution. The government is also promoting reduction and recycling of waste and aims to achieve a recycling rate of 50 per cent by 2010.

# CHAPTER 6

# ✡ Changing Relationships

I srael's association with other countries has often been tense. There have been many criticisms of its policies towards the Palestinians and its building of Jewish settlements in the occupied territories. The international community does not recognize Israel's 1967 annexation of East Jerusalem, the West Bank and the Gaza Strip, and a majority of UN members do not accept Israel's assertion in 1980 that Jerusalem "complete and united" is its capital. For this reason, almost all foreign embassies in Israel are based in Tel Aviv. Despite these disagreements, Israel currently has good diplomatic relations with 163 out of the

**Demonstrators in Istanbul, Turkey, burn an Israeli flag in protest at the assassination of a Hamas leader by Israeli forces in March 2004. Israel's policy of targeted killings of militant Palestinian leaders has been condemned by much of the international community.**

world's 191 countries. Most of those nations that do not recognize Israel are Muslim states.

## Arab and Muslim states

In 1945, the Arab League Council declared a formal boycott of any Jewish-owned business operating in Palestine. All Arab institutions, organizations, merchants and individuals were called upon 'to refuse to deal in, distribute or consume Zionist products or manufactured goods'. The Organization of the Islamic Conference (OIC), formed in 1969 from 24 Islamic states, has pressured its members to refuse trade with Israel and campaign for Israel's withdrawal from the occupied territories. Israel is excluded from membership of the OIC and the Arab League.

Israel's diplomatic isolation among Arab countries began to end in 1979, when it signed a peace treaty with Egypt. Under the treaty's terms, both countries agreed to recognize each other and end the state of war that had existed between them since 1948. Israel further agreed to withdraw from the Sinai Peninsula, captured in 1967, and Egypt permitted Israeli shipping access to the Red Sea and Indian Ocean via the Suez Canal, the Gulf of Aqaba and the Strait of Tiran. Israel signed a further peace treaty with Jordan in 1994, which stabilized relations between the two countries and resolved territorial and trade disputes between them. As a result of the peace process with the PLO in the 1990s, Israel established or renewed diplomatic relations with many other countries, both Muslim and non-Muslim.

However, relations between Israel and its neighbouring countries to the north, Lebanon and Syria, remain strained. Israel invaded Lebanon in 1982, following PLO attacks on its northern towns launched from there. Israel maintained a small force in southern Lebanon until 2000. Since then, the Lebanese-based Shia group Hezbollah, with support from Iran and Syria, has strengthened its hold over the region. Hezbollah fighters attacked some Israeli soldiers in July 2006, prompting Israel to launch air strikes against southern Lebanon. Israel's bombing raids on Hezbollah strongholds caused heavy casualties, especially among civilians. Hezbollah responded with rocket attacks on Israel's cities. Israel failed to defeat Hezbollah, and its northern border remains a potential flashpoint for future conflict.

Negotiations between Israel and Syria during the 1990s failed to produce an agreement. Israel's continued occupation of the Golan Heights remains a major stumbling block to peace between the two nations.

## Allies of Israel

Israel has historically close ties with the USA, which was the first country to recognize the founding of the state of Israel in 1948. The USA views Israel as a key strategic ally in the Middle East, and Israel has been one of the major recipients of US military and economic aid. The USA is Israel's leading trading partner. Israel also has strong historic relations with Armenia, due in part to the Armenian community of Jerusalem.

### FOCUS: EMERGENCY HEALTH CARE

Israel's experience on the front line of a long-term conflict has given the country's medical system a great deal of experience with emergency health care, an expertise they have been keen to share with other countries. Israeli hospitals have developed advanced techniques for dealing with severe burns and injuries and Israeli medical experts have always been quick to fly anywhere in the world to help in the event of disasters such as earthquakes.

**The UN Secretary-General Ban Ki-moon (right) meets with Dahlia Itzik, Speaker of the Israeli Knesset, at the UN Headquarters in New York in 2007 to discuss the peace process.**

New Zealand has been a long-term supporter of Israel, dating back to its approval of the 1947 UN partition plan. Perhaps surprisingly, Turkey is another very close ally, and was the first Muslim-majority nation to recognize the state of Israel. Their closeness may be explained in part by their similarities: both are Western-style liberal democracies based in the Middle East. Finally, Israel has strong historical, commercial and cultural relations with Europe, from where many Israelis trace their origins.

## International organizations

Israel is a member of a number of international organizations, including the United Nations, the

World Health Organization and the International Atomic Energy Agency. Israel also plays a full part in the global economy and has free trade agreements for industrial goods with the European Union (since 1975) and the USA (since 1985). Israel also participates in the UN Conference on Trade and Development (UNCTAD), the International Bank for Reconstruction and Development, the World Bank, the International Finance Corporation and the International Monetary Fund.

## The United Nations

Israel joined the United Nations (UN) in 1949. Since then, numerous UN resolutions have been passed criticizing Israeli actions. From 1967 to 1989, the UN passed 131 resolutions critical of Israel. For example, in 1975, the UN General Assembly passed a resolution (repealed in 1991) that declared Zionism to be a form of racism. Security Council Resolution 242, passed in 1967, called on Israel to withdraw from lands captured that year in exchange for peace with the Arab states. Resolution 242 has subsequently formed the basis of all peace talks between Israel and the Arabs, but there have been many disagreements about how it can be achieved. The main stumbling block for Israel is that it is unwilling to exchange land without guarantees of security.

UN resolutions have also been supportive of Israel. The 1947 UN partition plan created the state. The UN resolutions in 1967 and 1973 called upon Arab states to recognize Israel's right to exist, and in 1998 the UN stated that anti-Semitism was a form of racism. The UN has acted numerous times over the years to end hostilities. In August 2006, during a war between Israel and Lebanon, the UN passed Security Council Resolution 1701, which placed sufficient pressure on both sides to agree a ceasefire.

## International assistance

In 1958, Israel launched the Centre for International Cooperation, known as MASHAV, which is a short form of the Hebrew name. MASHAV's aim was to share with developing countries the knowledge and technologies that formed the basis for Israel's own rapid economic development. Since its modest beginnings, MASHAV has trained almost 200,000 people from approximately 140 countries in many areas of Israeli expertise. These include managing water resources and irrigation, desert farming and preventing desertification, emergency and disaster medicine, and helping the integration of immigrants through education and other programmes. MASHAV's priorities are to ease poverty, provide food security, empower women and improve basic health and education services. MASHAV offers almost 300 courses per year, both in Israel and abroad.

## Tourism

With its historical and religious sites, along with its warm, Mediterranean climate, Israel attracts a regular stream of tourists. Tourism tends to decline during periods of terrorist violence. In 2000, tourist numbers reached over two million, but after the second intifada began that year, Israel received less than a million visitors. Numbers slowly began to rise again thereafter, and in 2005 1,902,700 tourists visited Israel. More than half of Israel's visitors come from Western Europe; a fifth come from North America; 11 per cent from Eastern Europe; and 10 per cent from Asia. A large number of tourists are Christian pilgrims visiting Jerusalem, Bethlehem and Nazareth. Other popular destinations include the Dead Sea, Elat and the Mediterranean coast.

### CASE STUDY: ST JOHN EYE HOSPITAL

The St John Eye Hospital in Jerusalem was established specifically to treat eye diseases that are common among Palestinians. The majority of patients come from the West Bank, Gaza and East Jerusalem. Eye disease causing blindness is ten times more frequent in these places than in developed countries. Each year, nearly 40,000 patients are treated at the hospital or in its mobile clinics. The founding stimulus of the hospital was to improve the quality of medical provision to the Palestinian community, who have historically been less well served than Israelis. The hospital is open to all who need help, regardless of their religion or race.

## Immigration

A key factor in Israel's economic expansion and cultural development since 1948 has been its encouragement of immigration. The numbers of immigrants has fallen in recent years, but the number of people leaving Israel has also fallen. Between 1948 and 1968, 45 per cent of immigrants were from Europe and the USA and 55 per cent were from Asia and Africa. From 1968, Jews from the USSR began moving in, and since 1989 over 700,000 immigrants have arrived from Eastern European countries.

## The World Zionist Organization

Historically, two organizations have helped Jews around the world to settle in Palestine/Israel. These are the WZO and JAFI. The WZO, or World Zionist Organization, was founded in 1897 in Basle, Switzerland. Its primary aim, the establishment of a Jewish homeland in Palestine, was achieved in 1948. JAFI – the Jewish Agency for Israel – was founded in 1929 by the WZO to help people around the world deal with any difficulties involved in their immigration to Israel. Both the WZO and JAFI continue to assist Jews to move from their countries to Israel, to settle in once there and to find homes, education and employment. They also help to defend the rights of Jews worldwide.

**Female Israeli soldiers welcome French immigrants with Israeli flags as they arrive at Ben Gurion Airport, near Tel Aviv, on 25 July 2007. Some 600 French Jews emigrated to Israel that day.**

During the opening ceremony of the 16th Maccabiah Games in 2001, an Israeli woman runs with a flag through the stadium. On the verge of cancellation because of the on-going al-Aqsa intifada, the event attracted over 2,200 athletes from 46 countries.

## The Jewish Olympics

Towards the end of the 19th century, some young European Jews decided to form a world sports organization named after Judas the Maccabee, one of the greatest warriors in Jewish history. The first Jewish sports club was founded in 1895 in Turkey. Other clubs followed. The first Maccabiah Games were held in 1932 in Palestine. Fourteen nations and 390 athletes competed. The games were nicknamed the 'Jewish Olympics'. Since then the games have been held every four years under the sponsorship of the Maccabi Federation. The games are now held in Tel Aviv and are the third largest sporting event in the world, after the Olympics and the Commonwealth Games. Although mainly for Jewish athletes, Arab Israelis can also participate. The games are sanctioned by the International Olympic Committee and World Federation of Sports and they bring together Jewish athletes from around the world to compete in a variety of sports.

### FOCUS: ALIYAH AND YERIDA

*Aliyah* (ascent) is the Israeli term for Jewish immigration to Israel. Jewish emigration from Israel is called *yerida* (descent). Since the mid-1990s, there has been a large *aliyah* of South African, American and French Jews. The Bnei Menashe Jews from India, which were officially recognized in 2005 as descendants of one of the Ten Lost Tribes of Israel, slowly started their *aliyah* in the early 1990s. Organizations such as Nefesh B'Nefesh and Shavei Israel help with *aliyah* by providing financial aid and guidance on a variety of topics such as finding work, learning Hebrew and adapting to Israeli culture.

# CHAPTER 7

# ✡ Future Challenges

Israel's population has increased approximately eightfold since 1948. Although this has created a rich and diverse culture, it has also produced challenges in accommodating and integrating so many different communities and minimizing damage to the natural environment. Economic pressures for urban development are leaving towns without parks, gardens and play areas, essential for health and quality of life. Safeguarding precious land resources is a vitally important national challenge.

**An ibex stands on a rock in the Hai-Bar Arava Biblical Wildlife Reserve in the Negev. Since 1969, the reserve has been reintroducing animals mentioned in the Bible, including lions, crocodiles and bears, to Israel.**

This chart shows the number of mammals, birds, reptiles and fish that live in Israel, as well the numbers of species that are currently endangered. Israel's biodiversity has been threatened by several factors, including urban development, the break-up of habitats through road and fence building, the introduction of non-native species, unregulated hunting and fishing, and pollution.

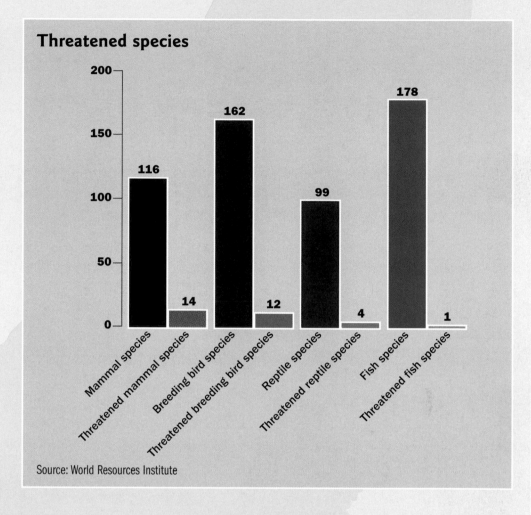

**Threatened species**

Source: World Resources Institute

It is predicted that if population growth continues at the current rate, within 30 years Israel could be the most densely populated country in the world. Conservation is an increasingly urgent issue.

## Conservation

For a small country, Israel has a rich variety of flora and fauna, with 2,317 plant varieties and 116 mammal species. Yet as it grows more urbanized, protecting this biodiversity becomes increasingly difficult. Since its foundation in

1953, the Society for the Protection of Nature in Israel (SPNI), along with the Nature Reserves Authority, has led dozens of campaigns to encourage people to care for Israel's environment. Today, the SPNI is Israel's largest non-governmental environmental organization, and nearly 20 per cent of Israelis are involved in some way in its programmes of education, conservation, research and action.

Laws have been passed to protect natural habitats, wildlife and sites of scientific and educational interest and there are now 155 nature reserves and national parks across Israel. Animals such as the leopard, gazelle, ibex and vulture have been declared protected species and are being assisted by the establishment of feeding stations and nesting sites.

### FORESTS AND PROTECTED LAND

Forested area as a per cent of total land area: 0.7%

Protected land areas as a per cent of total land area: 19.1 %

Number of protected areas in the country: 184

Source: Israel Ministry of Environmental Protection

In the early 1900s, Israel's woodland areas had been almost totally destroyed after centuries of forest clearance for farmland. By 1948, there were fewer than five million trees in the entire country. Today, over 200 million trees have been planted in an active reforestation programme led by the Jewish National Fund (JNF).

One of the most threatened environments in Israel is along the over-developed Mediterranean coastline. New towns, tourist resorts, mines and industrial developments have led to the extinction

**A desert flower wilts in the cracked, parched ground on the shore of the Dead Sea. This area of the shore used to be covered with water, but in recent years the water level has been dropping. This is partly due to a high rate of evaporation, and partly because the rivers that feed the Dead Sea have been diverted by Israel and Jordan for their water needs.**

of many species and the loss of nearly 70 per cent of Israel's Mediterranean beaches. Overuse of limited water resources and draining of marshes have destroyed many wetland areas and the species that live and grow there. In 2003, the government set up a National Biodiversity Strategy and Action Plan to deal with some of these concerns. This has helped to make the public more aware of the damage they were unconsciously doing to local ecosystems.

## Water shortages

The combination of severe water deficiency, contamination of existing water reserves, densely populated urban areas and highly intensive irrigated agriculture, makes it essential for Israel to increase its development and exploitation of all possible water resources.

Israel's water resources are limited. Seventy-five per cent of the annual rainfall is concentrated into four winter months. Rainfall is also unevenly distributed with averages of up to 950 mm a year in some parts of Galilee in the north compared to 25 mm in the southern Negev. In periods of drought, the situation becomes yet more serious. Because of this, Israel is already a world leader in recycling wastewater, with nearly 70 per cent of wastewater treated and reused for agricultural purposes, mainly for the irrigation of non-food crops and animal fodder.

While water scarcity and contamination remain major problems, experts believe that effective water quality management can be achieved with the cooperation of the public. Everyone is urged to save water and the advertising slogan 'Don't waste a drop' is known in every Israeli home. Water scarcity has long been a source of tension in the region and has sparked a number of skirmishes between Israel and its neighbours. Some water resources are shared, such as the Jordan River, shared by Lebanon, Jordan, Israel and Syria, and control of this waterway has been and continues to be a contentious issue. Before a lasting peace is possible in the region, all the countries involved will have to reach agreements over the preservation and sharing of water resources.

## Air quality

One consequence of Israel's rapid economic growth has been sharp rises in air pollutants emitted by factories and motor vehicles. Pollutants include suspended particulate matter, carbon dioxide, sulphur dioxide and nitrogen oxide. Reducing air pollution without harming economic development is a major challenge for the future. Several steps have already been taken in this direction. Since 1995 all new, imported cars are equipped with catalytic converters and use unleaded petrol. The government has also restricted the use of private cars in city centres, improved the efficiency of public transport, pressured industries to lower their emissions of pollutants, funded research into alternative fuels and provided educational programmes to encourage environmental awareness.

## PROJECTED WATER SUPPLY AND DEMAND

| Year | Population (million) | Water sources (million cubic metres) | | | | | |
| | | Surface water | Ground water | Brackish | Treated effluents | Desalination | Total |
| --- | --- | --- | --- | --- | --- | --- | --- |
| 2010 | 7.4 | 645 | 1050 | 165 | 470 | 100 | 2,430 |
| 2020 | 8.6 | 660 | 1075 | 180 | 565 | 200 | 2,680 |

Source: Israel Water Commission

## The conflict

Achieving a lasting peace with the Palestinians remains one of Israel's most significant challenges. In recent years, Palestinian loyalties have been split between two organizations, the Islamist group Hamas and the secular nationalist party Fatah, the largest faction of the PLO. The Hamas-Fatah split has impeded progress in the peace process.

In 2005, Israel took the unilateral step of withdrawing its troops from Gaza and dismantling its 21 settlements there, while retaining control of the territory's air space and borders. In January 2006, Hamas beat Fatah in the elections for the Palestinian Legislative Council, elevating the group – which did not recognize Israel's right to exist and had engaged in long-term terrorist activity – to a position of authority. In 2007,

following a brief war with Fatah, Hamas seized control of Gaza. With Hamas continuing to refuse to recognize Israel, hopes for peace have become focused on negotiations with the more moderate Fatah government in charge of the West Bank.

## Issues dividing the two sides

Since the 1993 Oslo Accords, both Israel and the Palestinians have been officially committed to finding a 'two-state solution' to the conflict by which both peoples can live side-by-side in territories with mutually recognized borders. One major problem has been in deciding exactly what those borders should be. Israel has accepted that

**In August 2005, Israeli soldiers evacuated Jewish settlers from the Gaza Strip. Here, a Jewish woman and her child are escorted by soldiers from their home in the settlement of Neve Dekalim.**

**Palestinian and Israeli children play football together during the first Japanese-Israeli-Palestinian Children's Friendship Soccer Match, held in Tokyo in August 2003. Initiatives such as this help to foster stronger links between the two communities.**

Gaza and the Palestinian-dominated areas of the West Bank should form part of a future Palestinian state. Israel insists, however, that Jerusalem should remain its 'eternal and undivided capital'. Religious and conservative Israeli groups are opposed to the return of any land to the Palestinians.

The Palestinians, on the other hand, claim entitlement to the whole of the West Bank, including the areas currently occupied by Jewish settlements, and Gaza, and East Jerusalem, where they hope to establish their capital. Groups such as Hamas and Hezbollah believe the Palestinian state should simply replace the state of Israel, which they say has no right to exist. Another divisive issue is the so-called 'right of return'. Palestinians insist that the descendants of the refugees who left their homes when Israel was established in 1948 should be permitted to return. Israel has consistently refused to allow this, partly because such a large-scale migration would threaten Israel's identity as a Jewish state.

## Hopes for peace

It is clear that the issues that divide the two sides are many and great. Yet most Palestinians and Israelis continue to support the peace process. Undoubtedly any final resolution will involve painful concessions for both peoples and may prompt a violent response from the extremists on either side. However, for many people, the ultimate goal of an Israel and a Palestine living peacefully side by side would be worth the struggle.

Israel, a young nation with an ancient heritage, has made dramatic progress since it was founded in 1948. Its future security and prosperity depends on its ability to cope with the consequences of that progress and to live in peace with its neighbours.

# Timeline

**May 1948** Declaration of the founding of the state of Israel. Neighbouring Arab states invade.

**1948** El Al, Israel's national airline, is founded.

**1948-9** 726,000 Palestinian Arabs become refugees.

**1950** The Knesset passes the Law of Return, allowing any Jew to settle in Israel.

**July-Oct 1956** Suez War

**1958** MASHAV is founded.

**1964** Israel completes its National Water Carrier project.

**June 1967** Six-Day War.

**October 1973** Yom Kippur War.

**Mar 1979** Israel and Egypt sign a peace treaty.

**1981** Israel formally annexes East Jerusalem and the Golan Heights.

**Jun–Aug 1982** Israel invades Lebanon and lays siege to Beirut, forcing the PLO to leave Lebanon.

**1987–1993** The first intifada.

**1990s** Almost a million Jews from the former Soviet Union emigrate to Israel.

**1991** The Middle East peace process begins with a conference in Madrid.

**Sept 1993** The Oslo Accords between Israel and the PLO are signed in Washington.

**1994** Israel signs a peace treaty with Jordan.

**1996** Israel launches its first satellite, AMOS.

**1994–1999** Israeli forces begin to withdraw from the West Bank, but peace process stalls.

**May 2000** Israel completes its withdrawal from Lebanon.

**2000-2005** Second intifada.

**Apr-Jun 2002** Israeli forces invade and reoccupy seven West Bank towns.

**Jun 2002** Israel begins construction of a 'security fence' around the Palestinian-controlled areas of the West Bank.

**Apr 2003** Launch of a 'road map to peace', a UN-backed plan to bring peace to the Middle East.

**Aug 2005** Israel dismantles the Jewish settlements in the Gaza Strip.

**June 2006** Israel invades Gaza.

**Jul-Aug 2006** War between Israel and Hezbollah fought in southern Lebanon and northern Israel.

**2007** Hamas defeats Fatah in a short war over control of Gaza.

# Glossary

**arable** Land that is suitable for growing crops.

**boycott** A form of protest involving the refusal to purchase from someone or to do business with them. In international affairs a boycott most often takes the form of refusal to import a country's goods.

**coalition** A union of different groups or parties who come together for a common purpose, for example to form a government.

**conscription** Compulsory military service.

**democratic** Describing a political system in which the people elect their own leaders.

**desertification** The transformation of land once suitable for agriculture into desert. Desertification can result from climate change or from human practices such as deforestation and overgrazing.

**deport** Force to leave a country.

**Diaspora** The scattering of Jews from Palestine to different places around the world.

**diplomatic relations** Formal dealings and associations between states.

**expatriate** A person who lives in a country other than his or her own.

**free enterprise** The freedom of private businesses to operate competitively, for profit, and without government controls.

**Hamas** An organization formed in 1987 that wishes to replace Israel with an Islamist Palestinian state. It is regarded as a terrorist organization by Israel, the United States and the European Union.

**Hezbollah** A Shi'ite Islamist political organization based in Lebanon that wishes to impose Islamic rule in Lebanon and eliminate Israel. Hezbollah, which means 'Party of God', has used terrorist tactics in its fight against Israel.

**Holocaust** The systematic extermination of nearly six million Jews by the Nazis during World War II.

**immigrant** A person who leaves one country to settle permanently in another.

**intifada** The Palestinian uprising in the occupied territories that took place between 1987 and 1993. A second intifada occurred between 2000 and 2005.

**irrigation** The artificial application of water to crops.

**Islamic Jihad** A militant group widely regarded as a terrorist organization. Its goal is the destruction of the state of Israel and its replacement with an Islamic state run by Palestinian Arabs.

**kibbutz** A commune in Israel, especially for farming, in which the residents own the wealth and property collectively.

**kosher** Describing food that has been prepared so that it adheres to Jewish dietary laws.

**moshav** A farming community in Israel in which each family works its land and lives separately while co-operating in the buying of equipment and supplies and in the marketing and selling of produce.

**occupied territories** Territories conquered by Israel in the 1967 Six-Day War. They included the Sinai Peninsula, the West Bank, the Gaza Strip and the Golan Heights. The Sinai Peninsula was returned to Egypt in 1979 and the Gaza Strip was handed to the Palestinian National Authority in 2005. Since 1993, parts of the West Bank have been placed under Palestinian civilian control while remaining under Israeli military control.

**Ottoman Empire** A Turkish empire established in the late thirteenth century in Asia Minor, eventually extending through the Middle East, which came to an end in 1918.

**refugees** A person who seeks refuge, especially from war or persecution, by going to a foreign country.

**semi-arid** Land that experiences little rainfall and has scrubby vegetation.

**terrorism** The deliberate use, or threat, of violence against civilian targets in pursuit of a political aim.

**welfare state** A system in which the government assumes the primary responsibility for assuring the basic health and financial wellbeing of its citizens.

# Further information

## Books

*Atlas of Conflicts: The Arab-Israeli Conflict* by Alex Woolf (Watts, 2004)

*Atlas of World Faiths: Judaism* by Cath Senker (Watts, 2007)

*Causes and Consequences: Arab-Israeli Conflict* by Stewart Ross (Evans, 2004)

*Eyewitness Travel Guide to Jerusalem and the Holy Land*, Ed. Kate Poole (Dorling Kindersley, 2000)

*Food and Festivals: A Flavour of Israel* by Ronne Randall (Wayland, 2002)

*Insight Guide: Israel* ed. Pam Barrett (Discovery Channel, 1999)

*World in Focus: Israel* by Alex Woolf (Wayland, 2007)

## Websites

news.bbc.co.uk/1/hi/world/middle_east/country_profiles/803257.stm
A profile of Israel and the Palestinian territories.

www.cia.gov/cia/publications/factbook/geos/is.html
Facts and figures about Israel.

www.economist.com/countries/Israel/
A profile of Israel and its economy.

www.historycentral.com/NationbyNation/Israel/Geo.html
Information on all aspects of Israel, including its government, geography, history and people.

www.mfa.gov.il/mfa
Information about all aspects of Israel from the Ministry of Foreign Affairs.

www.science.co.il/Israel-info.asp
Information about Israel from the Israel Science and Technology Homepage.

www.sviva.gov.il
Information about the environment and conservation in Israel from the Ministry of the Environment.

www.who.int/countries/isr/en/
Information about health in Israel.

# Index